Little Rose © 2022 by Jel (Janall Mok)

Printed in the United States of America

U.S. trade bookstores and wholesalers: Please contact Janall by email.

PoetryByJel@gmail.com

Twitter: @JellyMok

Instagram: @PoetryByJel

Cover book by Jel (Janall Mok)

Acknowledgments

Dreams can be scary to pursue but with support and
love like those in my life, one can become better.

My Parents

Francis A. Mok and Patricia Mok

My Best Friends

Brandon Burton and Leeroy J. Sterling

My Girl Crew

Caitlin Emerson   Allison DiVerde

Kelsey Hartland

Corissa Schrade   Carolyn Wilson

Jennifer Rodriguez

Megan Randby   Kirsten Berlet

Time goes by

Faster than lightning strikes

In a blink of an eye

A lifetime's passed by

These short poems are accompanied with a singular line, a lingering thought.

Just as each petal on a rose is beautiful on its own, these short poems hold their own individual beauty.

But each petal is capable of becoming more when they are brought together.

Table of Contents

A Thousand Miles from Land   2

Your Voice   4

Midnight Sky   6

A Million Waves at Sea   8

Passion   10

Love is an Addiction   12

All I Can think About is You   14

What is it About You?   16

Magnificence   18

The Rose that Cannot Be   20

Roots   22

Nourish   24

My Problems are Bigger that this World   26

Battle Wounds   28

Darkness is Wisdom   30

This Ship Out on the Sea   32

Lost Time   34

Discovery   36

I Can't Help but Feel Worthless   38

Table of Contents

Blinded Love   40

Truth's Awakening   42

It Hurts, It Makes Me Weak   44

Fragile Heart   46

Guiding Light   48

There You Are, Little Rose   50

Angels   52

Something More   54

As Tempting as Can Be   56

Work of Art   58

Apple Pie   60

I Want to Cherish You and Hold You   62

Be Still   64

Quiet Night   66

To Feel Your Heart Beat   68

Falling Sky   70

Energy   72

Your Thorns Are Razor Sharp   74

The Burning Sky   76

Table of Contents

Searching for Light 78

They Hurt, They Make Me Weep 80

Journey 82

Should I Bleed For You? 84

Spirit 86

Keep Fighting 88

Should I Let You Bleed? 90

Choice 92

Troublesome Deed 94

You Don't Want to Leave Your Roots 96

Do Not Worry 98

Are You Who You Want to Be? 100

You're Afraid of Letting Go 102

I Am Still Falling In Love With You 104

Dove 106

Petals Were Torn from You, Little Rose 108

Grow, Little Rose 110

Unity 112

You Shouldn't Grow 114

Table of Contents

Mother Earth   116

Bravery   118

Bloom, Little Rose   120

Stars   122

Remain Strong   124

Let Your Velvet Petals Free   126

Shed Your Skin   128

Guiding Voice   130

You are the Most Beautiful Rose   132

Beauty   134

Flower in the Snow   136

My Eyes Have Come to See   138

Think of Me   140

Equal Value   142

Maybe I'll Write Our Story One Day   144

Nothing Special   149

Little Rose   155

It seems we are back where we started, Little Rose.

A Thousand Miles from Land

A thousand miles from land

But my heart remains close to you

So won't you take my hand

And let this love sing to you

Your words dance in my mind.

Your Voice

Your voice

Speaks to me

Like a song's

Sweet melody

Memories stumble upon me, like a childhood song.

Midnight Sky

Your eyes

Shine as bright

As the stars

In the midnight sky

We arrived where our paths met as one.

A Million Waves at Sea

A million waves at sea

Can shield you from the night

Proving life can truly be

An extraordinary sight

It draws me back to you, just as the moon craves the sun.

Passion

While in your company

I find passion

You give me something

I cannot fashion

Old moments are awoken by the beating of a drum.

Love is an Addiction

Love is an addiction

To escape from reality

Beginning with a simple touch

Then thrust into a reverie

Your past self begins to consume my mind.

All I Can Think About is You

All I can think about is you

How I wish it wasn't true

Seeing you as half of my heart

Makes this love a work of art

My eyes see that you are no longer that fragile cracked seed.

What is it About You?

Is it your smile?

Or maybe your voice

I think it's your eyes

Their softness, of course

My mind wanders like the mundane attempting to understand the divine.

Magnificence

You are magnificent to me

You laugh and cry

Proclaiming your love

Fearlessly

I can see that you have begun to grow your roots.

The Rose that Cannot Be

The rose that cannot be

With its velvet petals broken

Is it a tragedy?

Or is it truth rarely spoken

Yet, I know the stem has not yet broken the surface.

Roots

A rose's growth is slow

Its most important moments shrouded

For its beauty to truly show

Its roots must first be grounded

But left in the right conditions, there is no stopping a rose finding its purpose.

Nourish

Roots are nourished from the soil

The sun starts creeping through

They grip the earth like a coil

And a cycle begins anew

A shadow is cast upon the ground.

My Problems are Bigger than this World

My problems are bigger than this world

But I am desperate to be free

As free as a flag newly unfurled

Forever waving in the morning breeze

It stunts the roots' growth, frozen in the moment.

Battle Wounds

I have accumulated battle wounds

Throughout significant times in my life

But the ones that hurt the most

Have not been made with knives

Those who cannot see, sully the soil's surroundings.

Darkness is Wisdom

As we grow into our lives

We see more of the world's darkness

As the light is extinguished from inside

Hope becomes hard to harness

The clouds have come, yet the soil remains dry.

This Ship out on the Sea

This ship out on the sea

Is just our love in the night

Just as winds lift a plane

We take oceanic flight

We become a sail in still water.

Lost Time

Unspoken words

Can always be said

But lost time

Will forever remain dead

Our minds are frozen with time itself.

Discovery

Seek comfort to know

That all was once discovered

Amongst the few

That dove into the unknown

Simple growth becomes an arduous wonder.

I Can't Help but Feel Worthless

I can't help but feel worthless

I'm not able to protect your light

I'm searching to find my purpose

But the end's still not in sight

The sunlight is no longer felt.

Blinded Love

Your love was blind when we first met

But your mind knows the truth

That there was darkness

Beyond our sunset

We run our ways through the veils of time as we witness chaos.

Truth's Awakening

Our love began to melt

And the seasons began to change

Mother's Earth's presence was felt

In the truth's brand-new awakening

How can this pain disorient one so much?

It Hurts, It Makes

Me Weak

It hurts, it makes me weak

Crosses my mind life a familiar sound

Because love isn't meant to be chased

It is only meant to be found

These old nightmares find their place as my heart begins to melt.

Fragile Heart

Love makes the heart fragile

As fragile as glass can be

Till its eventual break

Broken for all eternity

Pain will always find a way to resurface, if not properly dealt.

Guiding Light

Always know

If the world becomes unkind

You will be your own guiding light

When darkness invades your mind

In what feels like eternal pain, mere seconds go by.

There You are, Little Rose

There you are, Little Rose

Sculpting your serendipity

But these challenges you forget to face

Are tied to your own agony

The stem is intact but the pain's kept inside.

Angels

Your existence in this world

Is proof enough

That there are angels

Which walk amongst us

Failing to make our past, present and future coincide.

Something More

I used to believe

Love was some folklore

But now I know

It was meant to give you more

Thorns have made their mark, like a weed, they infest.

As Tempting as Can Be

As tempting as can be

Expectations are a thief

This loves not meant for me

But you will always believe

We attempt to flee these flaws once more.

Work of Art

These waves of passion

Come crashing through my heart

As I feel the beat of your love

Speaking to me like a work of art

Balancing the past and present like an impossible test.

Apple Pie

Just you and me

And apple pie's subtle scent

But if it wasn't meant to be

And we were just meant as friends

Then I would be just as content

The forgotten thorns have found their form.

I Want to Cherish You and Hold You

I want the cherish you and hold you

So you can finally grow

Seeing what you've been through

I hope you'll always know

These thorns come out to play.

Be Still

Be still

For when you open your eyes

You will soon come to realize

Your mind yet carries

Free will

As our blissful ignorance has us run away.

Quiet Night

Here's to the quiet nights

That I spent with you

Holding you tight

Observing the company of few

The stillness of the night fills the air with doubt.

To Feel Your Heart Beat

Each beating of your heart

Sings like an open drum

Becoming a harmony

Beating in unison

The infestation spreads like a disease

Falling Sky

The warmth of the fireplace

Where we watch the falling sky

On a cold winter's night

We create our own type of high

The past with present keeps the petals from blooming
out.

Energy

To feel the softness of your skin

And to hear the beating of your heart

Fuels my life from within

Giving me a brand-new start

With the past becomes the present, time takes its toll.

Your Thorns are Razor Sharp

Your thorns are razor sharp

I feel I'm bleeding out

They're wrapped around my heart

And filling me with doubt

Old wound reappears like a sinkhole.

The Burning Sky

The burning sky

Quite the wonderous sight

But I could have never imagined

It would consume all the sunlight

Trying to keep our petals whole.

Searching for Light

We start out as children

Hopeful and always doing what's right

And end as adults

Desperately searching for the light

We try to find an out as the wound's cut deep.

They Hurt, They Make Me Weep

They hurt, they make me weep

Your thorns are here to stay

I wanted to be free

But I got in my own way

Making a choice, if we want to grow.

Journey

The journey

Does not need to be

If it does not

Make you happy

The past in the present, we cannot keep.

Should I Bleed for You?

Should I bleed for you?

To help your pain find its home

Pain can be healed by two

But it may prevent your growth

The roots aren't meant to surface.

Spirit

You devastated me

You gave me all this pain

But you showed me something more

Permission to love myself again

It prevents the rose's growth.

Keep Fighting

If you find you dim your light

For your lover to shine

Then you are drowning yourself

And hiding, when you need to fight

The past will not help these petals grow.

Should I Let You Bleed?

Should I let you bleed?

This pain is hard to bear

Your darkness is a weed

It's spreading everywhere

A decision must be made.

Choice

I can see it in your eyes

And hear it in your voice

You do not want this path

As it is not your own choice

A clear choice from an outside view.

Troublesome Deed

Having what you need

Needing what you want

Proves to be a troublesome deed

That may never be won

These thorns are now part of me, they formed as I grew.

You Don't Want to Leave
Your Roots

You don't want to leave your roots

As life is ever fleeting

But when we learn to solve disputes

Change becomes a different greeting

We focus on the thorns.

Do Not Worry

We struggle to find our way

On the cusp of new beginning

But focus too much on the day

And you will have lost the morning

Yet, our petals keep falling out

Are You Who You Want to Be?

We lose who we want to be

When stuck in the stems of our past

Letting go will help us see

That growth can truly last

Our focus turns askew as we start to form our doubt

You're Afraid of Letting Go

You're afraid of letting go

The pain has drained your light

How could you ever know

What was beyond your line of sight

It's time we let go the past.

I am Still Falling in Love with You

My heart wishes it wasn't true

But I am still falling in love with you

And after all this time a part

I still see you as a work of art

We watch our velvet petals fall down.

Dove

A heart filled with love

A mind clouded by doubt

Will clip the wings of a dove

And fill the sky with clouds

But the pain makes us ask, "Is there another way out?"

Petals Were Torn from You, Little Rose

Petals were torn from you, Little Rose

You fear you're losing beauty

But your fears are your own foes

They're your own form of self-cruelty

The answer sings that there is no other way

Grow, Little Rose

Remain Strong, Little Rose

For it won't be long

Until your life truly grows

We must come to terms with our past.

Unity

Lead with unity

And never fear loss

For there is beauty

Amidst the chaos

Lest we want the pain to stay.

You Shouldn't Grow

You shouldn't try to grow

Your fallen petals

Learn to let them go

And never settle

Honor our journey, Little Rose.

Mother Earth

Mother Earth is so bold

To be able to shed her skin

For her own reasons

In what we call seasons

Make peace with your past.

Bravery

Where hate divides

Love unites

Where fear restricts

Bravery persists

Running away from your own thorns will never last.

Bloom, Little Rose

Bloom, Little Rose

Don't ever hide your might

For a rose cannot grow

Without both rain and sunlight

This pain is rooted like a weed in the grass.

Stars

Reach for the stars

And see what you are destined for

Honor the past scars

But strive to achieve something more

Courage weakened, like the structure of a broken glass.

Remain Strong

For you are the flower in the snow

And I wish you would know

That in times you feel you might fall

You must stand strong and tall

But acceptance is essential for peace to last.

Let Your Velvet Petals Free

Let your velvet petals free

Rediscover your own light

The pursuit of happiness

Is always worth the fight

We gaze upon the nature-soaked earth.

Shed Your Skin

Little Rose

Shed your skin

And let a new

Life begin

Its soil freshly nourished.

Guiding Voice

Even with the world

In disarray

Your voice helps me

Find my way

The rose begins to show its velvet petals.

You are the Most Beautiful Rose

You are the most beautiful rose

And your thorns don't mean you're broken

So, keep all your precious thorns close

And pursue your dreams with full devotion

Thorns gently brushed from the morning dew.

Beauty

Little Rose

You have come back to me

In an evolved form more beautiful

Than my eyes have come to see

Clarity comes to fruition with the release of burdened

past.

Flower in the Snow

You are the sun rays through clouds

The rainbow in the rain

And even if you don't believe it

You are relief from a world of pain

The rose brought back through life seen anew.

My Eyes Have Come to See

My eyes have come to see

This love hid the broken

Your thorns captivated me

And let my love go unspoken

Honor your past and let go of those broken petals.

Think of Me

Think of me

During the still cold night

As the soft subtle snow

Glistens in the moonlight

Know your thorns hold beauty.

Equal Value

Some day

You will find someone

Who can cradle your thorns

Like a delicate dove

For this growth is meant to last.

Maybe I'll Write Our Story One Day

Maybe I'll write our story one day

A story of lovers who live far away

Whose hearts felt like home

But could never live as one

Your story isn't over…

Your journey is not yet done...

For the fragments of your story…

Tell a tale not yet sung…

It seems we are back where we started, Little Rose.

Your words dance in my mind. Memories stumble upon me, like a childhood song. We arrived where our paths met as one. It draws me back to you, just as the moon craves the sun. Old moments are awoken by the beating of a drum. Your past self begins to consume my mind. My eyes see that you are no longer that fragile cracked seed. My mind wanders like a mundane attempt to understand the divine. I can see that you have begun to grow your roots. Yet I know the stem has not yet broken the surface. But left in the right conditions, there is no stopping a rose finding its purpose.

149

A shadow was cast upon the ground. It stunts the roots' growth, frozen in the moment. Those who cannot see, sully the soil's surroundings. The clouds have come, yet the soil remains. We become a sail in still water. Our minds are frozen by time itself. Simple growth becomes an arduous wonder. The sunlight is no longer felt. We run our way through the veils of time as we witness chaos. How can this pain disorient one so much? These old nightmares find their place as my heart begins to melt. Pain will always find a way to resurface, if not properly dealt with.

In what feels like eternal pain, mere seconds go by. The stem is intact but the pain's kept inside. Failing to make our past, present and future coincide. Thorns have made

their mark, like a weed, they infest. We attempt to flee

these flaws once more. Balancing the past and the

present is like an impossible test. The forgotten thorns

have found their way. These thorns come out to play. As

our blissful ignorance has us run away. The stillness of

the night fills the air with doubt. The infestation spreads

like a disease. The past and present keep the petals from

blooming out.

As the past becomes the present, time takes its toll. Old

wounds reopen like a sinkhole. Trying to keep our petals

whole, we try to find an out as the wound cut deep.

Making a choice, if we want to grow. The past and the

present, we cannot keep. The roots aren't meant to

surface. It prevents a rose's growth. The past will not

help these petals grow. A decision must be made. The

choice is clear from an outside view. These thorns are

now part of me, they formed as I grew.

We focus on the thorns. Yet, our petals keep falling out.

Our focus turns askew as we start to form our doubts.

It's time we let go of the past. We watch our velvet petals

fall down. But the pain makes us ask, "Is there another

way out?" The answer sings that there is no other way.

We must come to terms with our past, lest we want the

pain to stay.

Honor our journey, Little Rose. Make peace with your past. Running away from your own thorns will never last. This pain is rooted like a weed in the grass. Courage weakened, like the structure of a broken glass. But acceptance is essential for peace to last.

We gaze upon the nature-soaked earth. Its soil is freshly nourished. The rose begins to show its velvet petals. Thorns gently brushed the morning dew. Clarity comes to fruition with the release of a burdened past. The rose brought back through life seen anew.

Honor your past and let go of those broken petals. Know

your thorns hold beauty. Because this growth is meant

to last.

Little Rose

A thousand miles from land

And a million waves at sea

All I can think about is you

The rose that cannot be

My problems are bigger than this world

Than this ship out on the sea

I can't help but feel worthless

It hurts, it makes me weak

So, there you are, Little Rose

As tempting as can be

I want to cherish you and hold you

And feel your heart beat

But your thorns are razor sharp

They hurt, they make me weep

Should I bleed for you?

Or should I let you bleed?

You don't want to leave your roots

Because you're afraid of letting go

But just because petals were torn from you Little Rose

Doesn't mean you shouldn't grow

So, bloom, Little Rose

Let your velvet petals free

Because you are the most beautiful Rose

That my eyes have come to see

Thank you for taking this journey, it will be worth it.

"To love is to know when to let go"